Lord it is good for us to be here.

Written by **Aileen Urquhart** ☆ Design by **Jelly** ☆ Illustration by **Louise Hilton** ☆
© 1999 Redemptorist Publications ☆ ISBN 0 85231 194 X ☆
Published by Redemptorist Publications, Alphonsus House, Chawton, Hampshire GU34 3HQ ☆www.redempt.org
A Registered Charity limited by guarantee. Registered in England 3261721
First Published May 1999   Second Printing June 1999 (20th thousand)

Nihil Obstat:
Canon Cyril Murtagh, M.A., S.T.L.
Censor Deputatus

Imprimatur: + Crispian Hollis
Episcopus Portus Magni
Portus Magni March 1999

3

WE ARE INVITED

I have come here today because God is my Father, and Jesus is my brother.

I have come here today because the Holy Spirit invites me.

THE PRIEST SAYS:
In the name of the Father and of the Son, and of the Holy Spirit

WE SAY:
Amen.

THE PRIEST SAYS:
The Lord be with you.

WE SAY:
And also with you.

Thank you God for inviting me to this M
I will try to give you my best love.
At this Mass I want to praise and thank :
for
M (tell God what you want to say thank you for)

☆ colour in David's missal

At this Mass I want to pray for
(tell God what you want to pray for)

4

OUR FATHER FORGIVES US - 1

It is so wonderful to be invited here.

God you are so good and kind.

I am sorry that I am not always good and kind.

THE PRIEST SAYS:
Lord, we have sinned against you:

WE SAY:
Lord have mercy.

THE PRIEST SAYS:
Lord, show us your mercy and your love:

WE SAY:
And grant us your salvation.

Sometimes the words are different.

THE PRIEST SAYS:
You were sent to heal the contrite:

WE SAY:
Lord have mercy.

THE PRIEST SAYS:
You came to call sinners:

WE SAY:
Christ have mercy.

THE PRIEST SAYS:
You plead for us at the right hand of the Father:

WE SAY:
Lord have mercy.

OUR FATHER FORGIVES US - 2

THE PRIEST SAYS:
May almighty God have mercy on us, forgive us our sins, and bring us to everlasting life.

WE SAY:
Amen.

THE PRIEST SAYS:
Lord have mercy.

WE SAY:
Lord have mercy.

THE PRIEST SAYS:
Christ have mercy.

WE SAY:
Christ have mercy.

THE PRIEST SAYS:
Lord have mercy.

WE SAY:
Lord have mercy.

Dear Father in heaven, thank you for your wonderful merciful love.
I am glad you forgive me when I
(Tell God something you're sorry about)

GOD IS SO WONDERFUL

When Jesus was born the angels sang this song. We all join in happily. In Advent and Lent this prayer is left out as these are very serious times.

Glory to God in the highest,
    and peace to his people on earth.
        Lord God, heavenly King,
            almighty God and Father,
                we worship you,
                we give you thanks,
            we praise you for your glory.
Lord Jesus Christ, only Son of the Father,
    Lord God, Lamb of God,
        you take away the sin of the world:
        have mercy on us;
you are seated at the right hand of the Father:
    receive our prayer.
        For you alone are the Holy One,
            You alone are the Lord,
                You alone are the Most High,
                Jesus Christ,
                with the Holy Spirit,
            in the glory of God the Father.
        Amen.

I will draw or write something I have seen or heard this week that makes me want to praise and thank God.

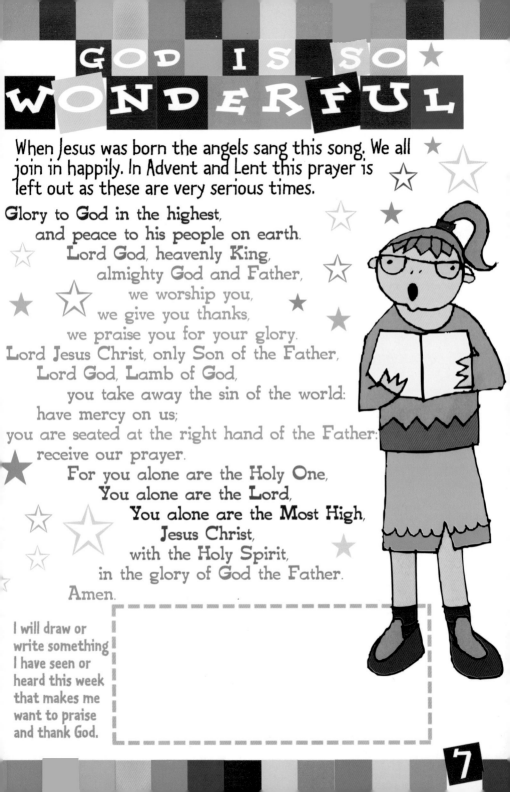

WE LISTEN TO GOD'S WORD -1

I listen to people who are important to me.
I listen to things I like.
So I will listen to the Word of God.

The First Reading

Before Jesus was born God spoke to people through holy men and women. God told the people to be kind to the poor and to strangers because God was kind to everyone.
Above all, God promised to send Jesus.

Today the first reading is about···

The Psalm

The psalm is a song to God. Sometimes the psalm praises God. Sometimes it asks God for help. Jesus learnt all the psalms when he was a boy. He loved to sing them.

Today the psalm is about···

The Second Reading

After Jesus had gone back to heaven his friends wrote letters about him. The letters remind us how wonderful Jesus was. Sometimes they say we are the brothers and sisters of Jesus, so we can be like Jesus too.

Today the second reading is about···

8

WE LISTEN TO GOD'S WORD -2

It is always exciting to hear good news.
The Gospel is the Good News which God gives us.
It is all about Jesus.

Sometimes it is a story that Jesus told us. Sometimes it is something that Jesus did. We stand up when we hear the Good News and we welcome the Gospel. Alleluia.

Dear Father in heaven, I will listen carefully to the Gospel.
Thank you for the Good News.

THE PRIEST SAYS:
The Lord be with you.

WE SAY:
And also with you.

THE PRIEST SAYS:
A reading from the holy gospel according to (Matthew, Mark, Luke or John)

WE SAY:
Glory to you, Lord.

Today's Gospel is about…

AFTER THE GOSPEL THE PRIEST SAYS:
This is the gospel of the Lord.

WE SAY:
Praise to you, Lord Jesus Christ.

WE HEAR MORE ABOUT THE READINGS

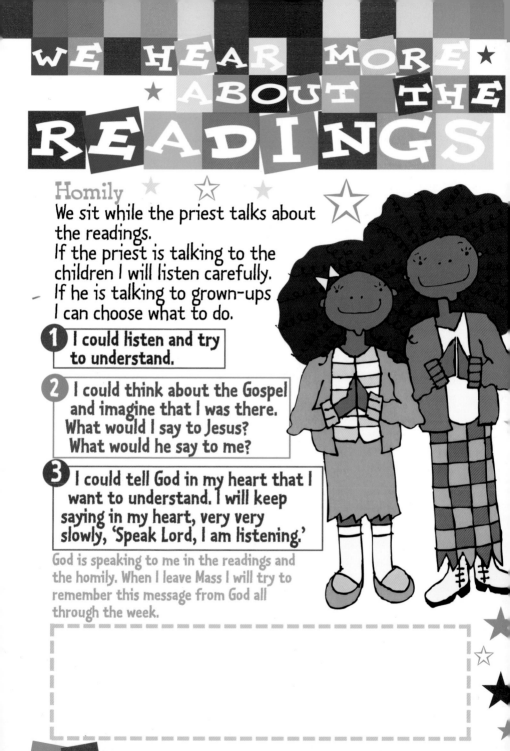

Homily

We sit while the priest talks about the readings.
If the priest is talking to the children I will listen carefully.
If he is talking to grown-ups I can choose what to do.

1 I could listen and try to understand.

2 I could think about the Gospel and imagine that I was there. What would I say to Jesus? What would he say to me?

3 I could tell God in my heart that I want to understand. I will keep saying in my heart, very very slowly, 'Speak Lord, I am listening.'

God is speaking to me in the readings and the homily. When I leave Mass I will try to remember this message from God all through the week.

DRAW A PICTURE OF THE GOSPEL

WE BELIEVE IN GOD AND THE CHURCH

We stand to proclaim our faith.

We believe in one God, the Father, the Almighty,
maker of heaven and earth,
of all that is, seen and unseen.
We believe in one Lord, Jesus Christ,
the only Son of God, eternally begotten of the Father,
God from God, Light from Light,
true God from true God, begotten, not made,
of one Being with the Father.
Through him all things were made.
For us men and for our salvation
he came down from heaven: (all bow)
by the power of the Holy Spirit
he became incarnate from the Virgin
Mary, and was made man.
For our sake he was crucified under
Pontius Pilate;
he suffered death and was buried.
On the third day he rose again
in accordance with the Scriptures:
he ascended into heaven
and is seated at the right hand of
the Father:
He will come again in glory to judge
the living and the dead, and his kingdom
will have no end.
We believe in the Holy Spirit, the Lord,
the giver of life,
who proceeds from the Father and the Son.
With the Father and the Son he is worshipped
and glorified.
He has spoken through the Prophets.
We believe in one, holy, catholic and
apostolic Church.
We acknowledge one baptism for the forgiveness of sins.
We look for the resurrection of the dead,
and the life of the world to come. Amen.

My God I believe in you, and all your Church teaches,
because you have said it, and your word is true.

WE PRAY FOR THE WHOLE WORLD

Bidding Prayers

Jesus tells us that God always listens to our prayers and gives us what is good for us.

I will pray for people in the church.
I will pray for people in other countries.
I will pray for people who help me.
I will pray for people who are poor or sad.
I will pray for myself.

Hail Mary, full of grace, the Lord is with you. Blessed are you among women, and blessed is the fruit of your womb, Jesus. Holy Mary, Mother of God, pray for us sinners, now and at the hour of our death. Amen.

Write down the names of people who need your prayers. If you can help them during the week write down what you can do for them.

O Lord hear my prayer.

13

WE BRING THE GIFTS TO THE ALTAR

We bring the bread, the wine and the money to the altar.
We need food, drink and money to stay alive.
We bring our lives to the altar.

THE PRIEST SAYS:

Blessed are you, Lord, God of all creation.
Through your goodness we have this bread to offer,
which earth has given and human hands have made
It will become the bread of life.

WE SAY:

Blessed be God forever.

THE PRIEST SAYS:

Blessed are you, Lord, God of all creation.
Through your goodness we have this wine to offer,
fruit of the vine and work of human hands. It will
become our spiritual drink.

WE SAY:

Blessed be God forever.

I offer you the hardest work I did this week. It was…

I offer you the happiest time I had this week. It was…

I offer you my sad times as well.
Help me to be brave.

14

WE ASK GOD TO TAKE OUR GIFTS

We have given God gifts of bread and wine, which take our place on the altar. We ask God to accept them.

THE PRIEST SAYS:

Pray, brethren, that our sacrifice may be acceptable to God, the Almighty Father.

WE SAY:

May the Lord accept the sacrifice at your hands, for the praise and glory of his name, for our good, and the good of all his Church.

We are praying for
a) God's glory — we want everyone to love him.
b) for our own good — we want to be good and happy.
c) for the Church — we want to spread the Good News.

THE PRIEST SAYS:

The Lord be with you.

WE SAY:

And also with you.

THE PRIEST SAYS:

Lift up your hearts.

WE SAY:

We lift them up to the Lord.

THE PRIEST SAYS:

Let us give thanks to the Lord our God.

WE SAY:

It is right to give him thanks and praise.

WE PRAISE GOD'S POWER AND MIGHT

Preface

The priest says a prayer of praise and thanks to God. This prayer changes at different times of the year. At Christmas the priest thanks God for sharing our life when he became a human being. At Easter he thanks God for the gift of everlasting life which Jesus gave us by his death and resurrection.

At this Mass I praise and thank God for...

EVERYONE THEN SINGS OR SAYS

Holy, holy, holy Lord, God of power and might, heaven and earth are full of your glory.
Hosanna in the highest.
Blessed is he who comes in the name of the Lord.
Hosanna in the highest.

THE EUCHARISTIC PRAYER

Most of the next part of the Mass is prayed by the priest. It changes from week to week. We join in silently.

I will listen carefully to what the priest is saying and join my prayers to his.

I may hear him pray for the Church — that is for the Pope, bishops, priests, and everyone who follows Jesus.

I pray for…

I may hear him pray for people who are alive.

I pray for someone who needs my prayers…

I may hear him pray for people who have died.

I pray for someone who has died…

I may hear him pray for everyone in church.

I pray for anything I need…

THE GIFTS BECOME JESUS OUR FOOD OF LIFE

The priest remembers what Jesus said and did at his Last Supper. He says and does the same.

JESUS SAID: Take
Eat
Take
Drink.

THE PRIEST SAYS: Take
Eat
Take
Drink.

I will hear a bell at this part of the Mass as it is so important. When the bell rings I will look up at the bread. It is now Jesus, the Bread of Life. Then I will look up at the wine. It is now Jesus, the Cup of Salvation.

This is me.
I give you my life.
As I gave myself for you on the cross.

WE SHOW OUR BELIEF

The bread and wine have been changed into Jesus.
This is the great mystery which we believe in.
To show our belief we say one of these prayers.

Christ has died.
Christ is risen,
Christ will come again.

or

Dying you destroyed our death,
Rising you restored our life,
Lord Jesus, come in glory.

When we eat this bread
and drink this cup,
we proclaim you death, Lord Jesus,
until you come in glory.

or

Lord, by your cross and resurrection
you have set us free,
You are the Saviour of the World.

The priest carries on praying for people
who need prayers, the living, the dead, for
all of us. He finishes this part of the Mass
with a very important prayer to the
Father, Son and Spirit.

THE PRIEST SAYS:

Through him, with him, in him, in the unity
of the Holy Spirit, all glory and honour is
yours, almighty Father, for ever and ever.

WE SAY:

AMEN

I will say it very loudly to show I have
joined my prayers with the priest's.

19

WE GET READY TO RECEIVE JESUS

We stand and say the Our Father with everyone.
We are all in God's family.
Our Father, who art in heaven,
  hallowed be thy name;
  Thy kingdom come; thy will be done
  on earth as it is in heaven.
 Give us this day our daily bread;
and forgive us our trespasses
as we forgive those who
trespass against us;
and lead us not into temptation,
but deliver us from evil.
The priest prays for peace as we wait for Jesus
to come again.
Then we all say
For the kingdom the power and the glory
are yours now and forever.
The priest asks us to show we are all one family.

THE PRIEST SAYS:
The Lord be with you.
WE SAY:
And also with you.
THE PRIEST SAYS:
Let us offer each other the sign of peace.

We give a loving sign to our family and friends.
The sign might be a kiss or a hand shake.

20

WE GET READY TO RECEIVE JESUS -2

WE ALL SING OR SAY TOGETHER:

Lamb of God, you take away the sins of the world: have mercy on us.
Lamb of God, you take away the sins of the world: have mercy on us.
Lamb of God, you take away the sins of the world: grant us peace.

THE PRIEST HOLDS UP THE BREAD OF LIFE AND TELLS US:

This is the Lamb of God, who takes away the sins of the world. Happy are those who are called to his supper.

WE SAY:

Lord, I am not worthy to receive you, but only say the word and I shall be healed.

We go to the altar and receive Jesus, the Food and Drink of Life.
Jesus, this is a very special time for us. I love you Jesus. I enjoy this quiet time. I will talk to you in my heart.

(If you are too young to go to Holy Communion you could draw a picture of the people in church and tell Jesus how much you want to have Holy Communion.)

WE GET READY TO GO OUT

The priest and altar servers clear away everything that was used for the Holy Meal. The altar is empty now, but the people in Church are filled with God's special gift of Jesus.

Jesus is with us and we are the Body of Christ.

THE PRIEST SAYS:

The Lord be with you;

WE SAY:

And also with you.

THE PRIEST SAYS:

May Almighty God bless you, the Father, the Son, and the Holy Spirit

WE MAKE THE SIGN OF THE CROSS ON OURSELVES AND SAY:

Amen.

Jesus asks us to carry on the work that he did on earth when he lived in Galilee. He asks us to spread his Good News to all the world.

THE PRIEST SAYS:

Go in the peace of Christ.
or: The Mass is ended, go in peace.
or: Go in peace to love and serve the Lord.

WE SAY:

Thanks be to God.